Bhishma's Vow

Subhadra Sen Gupta

Om Books International

A long, long time ago, there was a kingdom called Hastinapur. This rich and powerful kingdom was ruled by King Shantanu. He was married to River Goddess Ganga and they had a son named Devavrata.

One day, Ganga said to Shantanu, "Now that you have a son, it is time for me to return to Heaven."

"Why do you want to leave?" Shantanu asked in surprise.

"Because I am a river goddess and my place is in Swarga," said Ganga and she vanished, leaving Shantanu heartbroken.

One day, while hunting in the forest, Shantanu saw a young girl rowing a boat in the river and fell in love with her.

Shantanu thought, "Oh, what a beautiful girl! I think this young woman would be the right queen for Hastinapur."

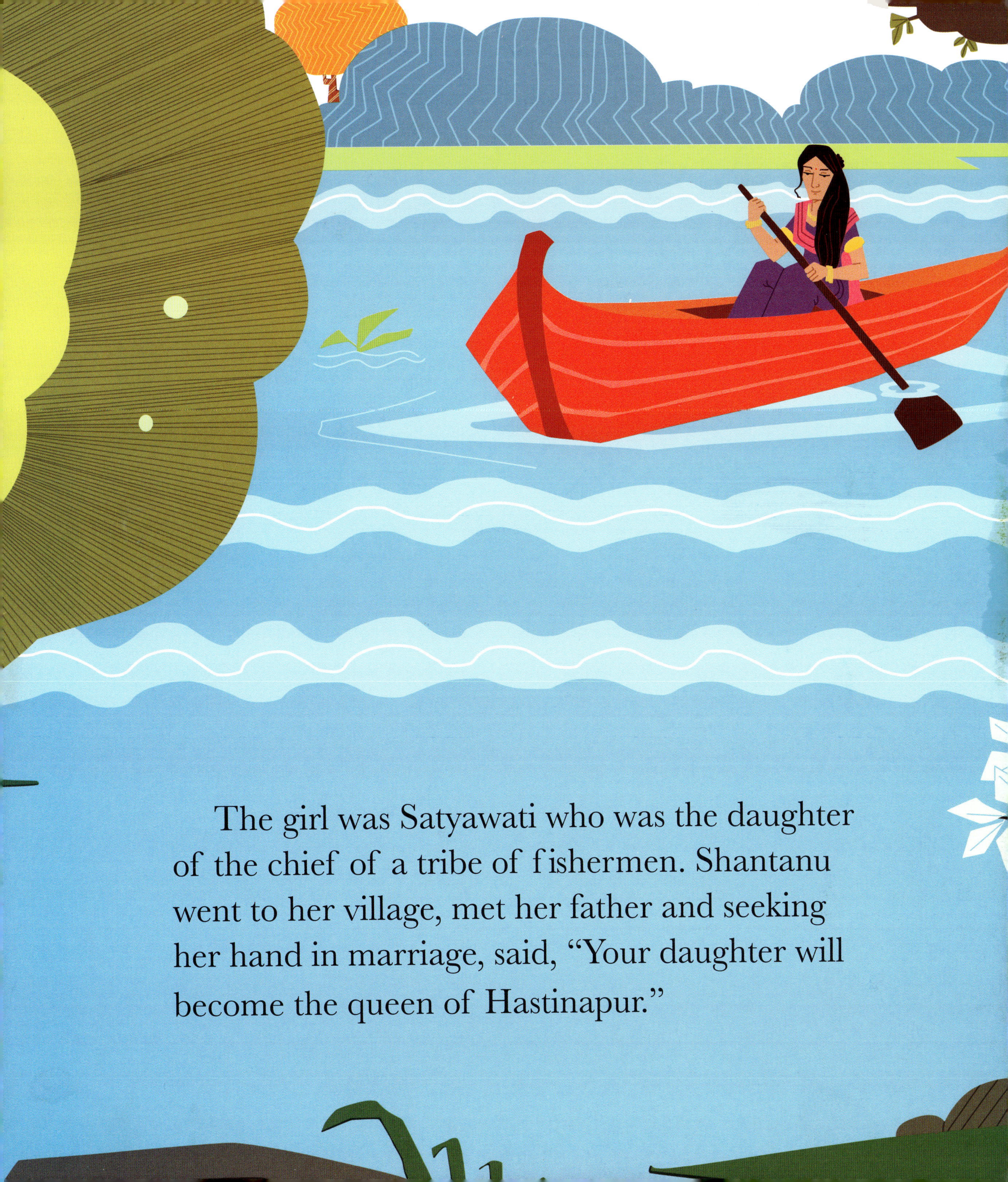

The girl was Satyawati who was the daughter of the chief of a tribe of fishermen. Shantanu went to her village, met her father and seeking her hand in marriage, said, "Your daughter will become the queen of Hastinapur."

Shantanu was surprised when Satyawati's father shook his head and replied, "That is not possible, Your Majesty. I have taken a vow that my daughter will marry a king only if her son becomes the heir apparent. You already have a son, Prince Devavrata, who will be the next king of Hastinapur."

“Also,” continued Satyawati’s father, “Devavrata is a young man and soon he will marry and have a son who will inherit the throne. Then what will my daughter and her children get? Satyawati will marry you only if you give the word that her son shall become the next king.”

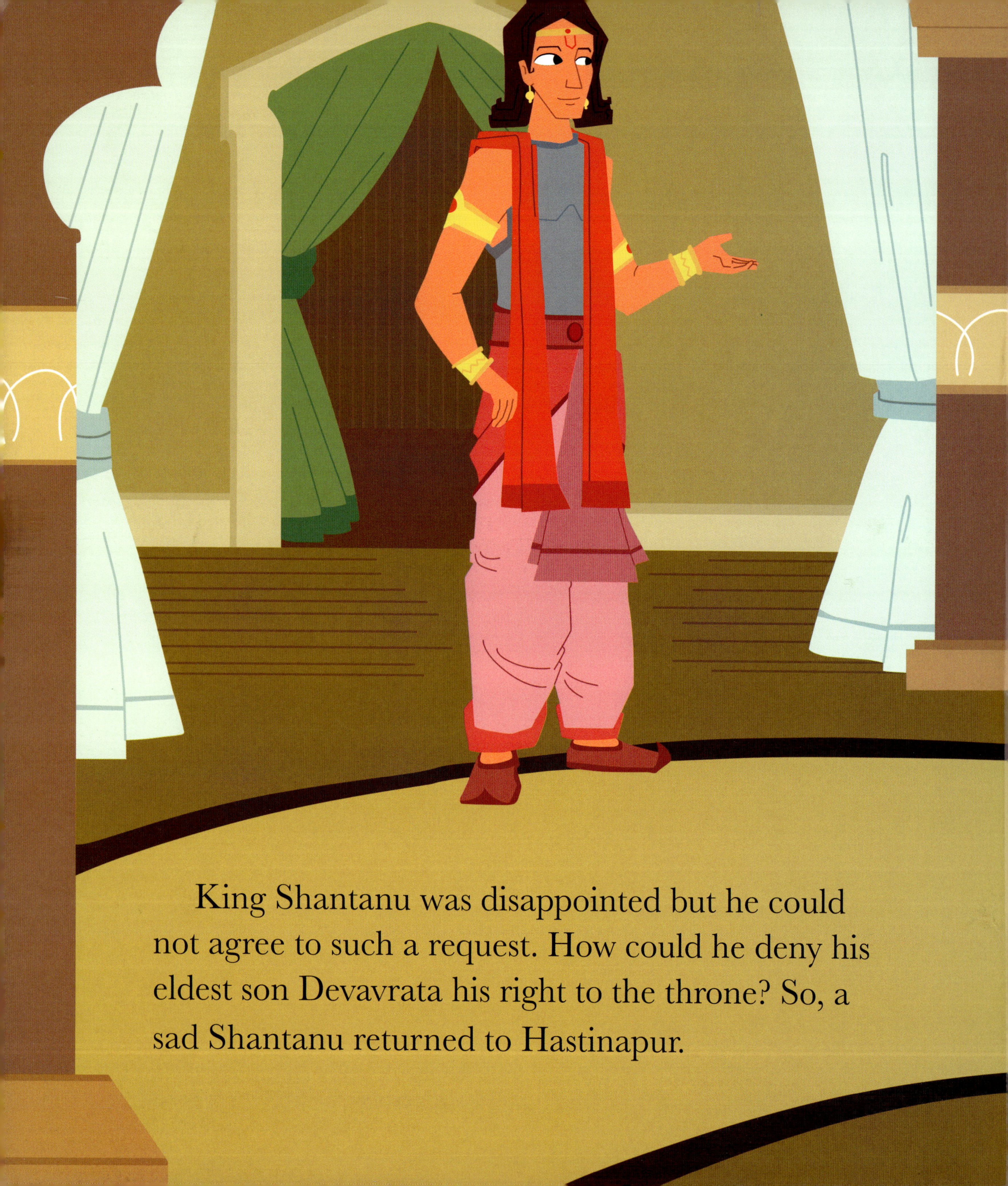

King Shantanu was disappointed but he could not agree to such a request. How could he deny his eldest son Devavrata his right to the throne? So, a sad Shantanu returned to Hastinapur.

Devavrata who was a brave and generous young man, looked at his father's worried face and asked, "Why are you so sad, Respected Father? Can I help you?"

Shantanu told him what Satyawati's father had said. "I cannot take away the throne from you, my son. So I cannot marry Satyawati."

Devavrata said, "Father, I take a vow! I will never sit on the throne of Hastinapur and I will never marry!" While everyone in the kingdom heard his words in stunned silence, he added calmly, "Prepare for the marriage of my father and Satyawati."

This was a 'bhishma', or a terrible vow, and that is why Devavrata began to be called Bhishma by the people.

Shantanu and Satyawati had two sons named Chitrangada and Vichitravirya. After the death of King Shantanu, Prince Chitrangada became the king but he too died soon after. When Vichitravirya followed his brother to the throne of Hastinapur, Bhishma felt it was time to get the young king married.

At this time, the king of Kashi was holding a swayamvara, a practice of choosing a life partner from among a list of suitors, for his three daughters–Amba, Ambika and Ambalika. All the kings were invited to the festivities where the princesses would select their husbands. However, the Kashi king did not invite the royal family of Hastinapur.

Angry and insulted at not being invited, Bhishma decided that the three princesses of Kashi would only marry Vichitravirya and no one else. So he rode up in his chariot to the swayamvara. Then, fighting off the soldiers, he carried them away to Hastinapur.

An angry Princess Amba refused to marry Vichitravirya as she had already chosen another king. She cursed Bhishma for carrying her away and said, "I curse you, Bhishma! One day I will be the reason for your death!"

Back in Hastinapur, Ambika and Ambalika were married to Vichitravirya. Now, Bhishma hoped that the sons of Vichitravirya would one day carry on with the royal duties of the kingdom. Sadly, he was to be disappointed.

Both Ambika and Ambalika gave birth to sons but there was no celebration in Hastinapur. Ambika's son named Dhritarashtra was born blind and Ambalika's son Pandu was pale and suffered from bad health. Soon after their birth, Vichitravirya died.

So Bhishma had to run the kingdom while Dhritarashtra and Pandu were growing up. Bhishma decided that Dhritarashtra could not become king because of his blindness. So Pandu was educated and trained in battle to be the next king.

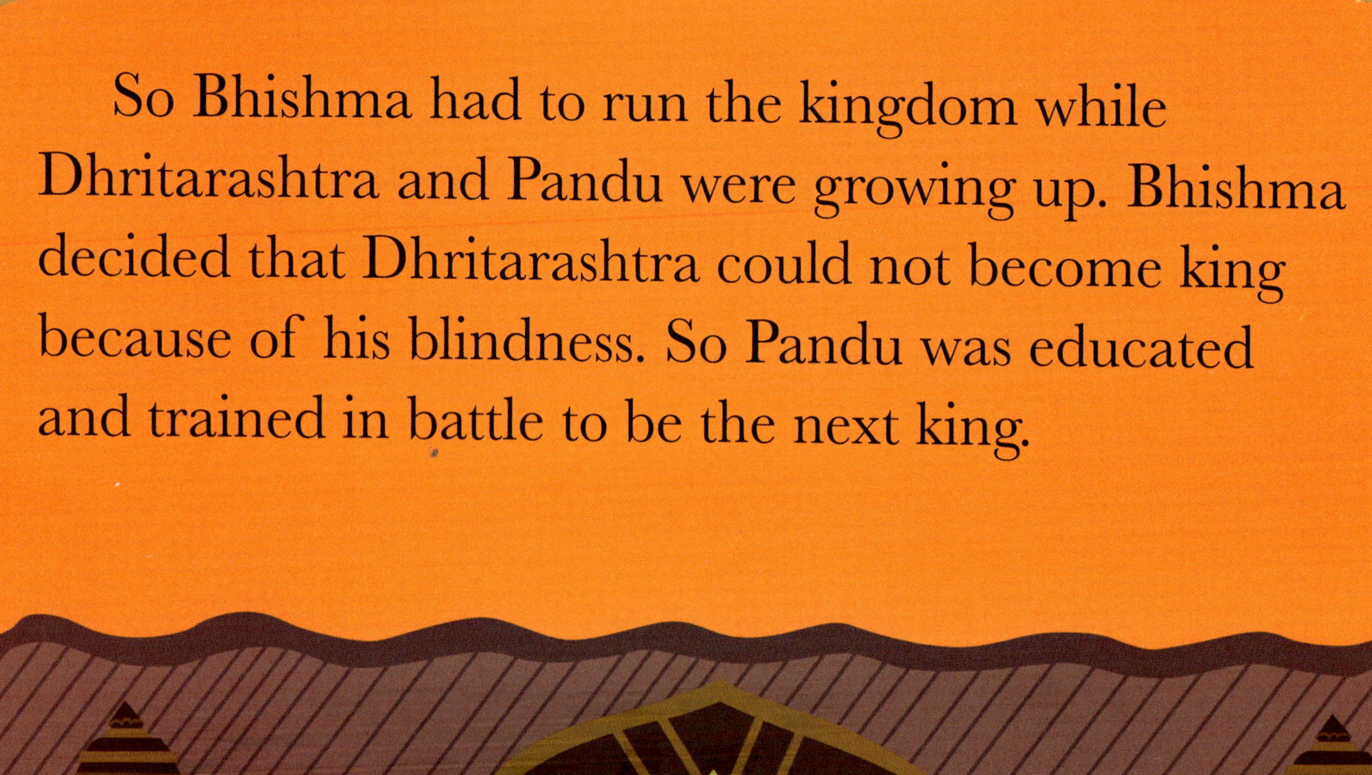